The Magic Well

A Comedy in One Act

by

Herman Ammann

I. E. CLARK, Inc.
Saint John's Road
Schulenburg, Texas 78956

THE MAGIC WELL

Cast

Old King Cole, a merry old soul
An Old Hag
An Old Man
An Old Woman
*The Town Poet
*The Town Fool
Mrs. Blinky, a nearsighted birdwatcher
Prince Arlo Marlowe, a professional hunter
Tissy, the pretty daughter of the king
Prissy, the clever daughter of the king
Lissy, the smart daughter of the king
*A Prologue
*A Dragon
A Frog

and, of course,

The Magic Well

Place: Way off somewhere
Time: You name it

[*May be played by men or women]

♦

"The Magic Well" was first presented at the 19th annual Schulenburg Theatre Festival on April 7 & 8, 1972, under the direction of Pat Castle of Texas A & M University with the following cast of junior high students:

Prologue	Robin Clark
The Dragon	Neal Richter
Old King Cole	Phil Lippman
Old Woman	Sheryl Simpson
Old Man	Mark Fitch
Town Poet	Michael Lebeda
Town Fool	Clay Rightmer
Old Hag	Glenda Getschmann
Mrs. Blinky	Susie Deterling
Prince Arlo Marlowe	Greg Mikesky
Tissy	Ginger Holub
Prissy	Debbie Frank
Lissy	Linda Valchar
Frog	Eddie Winkler

NOTES ON THE PLAY

"The Magic Well" is another of Herman Ammann's delightful plays for children of all ages. For those who are young in years, there's Old King Cole . . . *not* a very Merry Old Soul as the play begins. And there's a real live dragon, and three beautiful — er, well — *interesting* princesses; and a frog that has been bewitched and made to live in the well for a hundred years.

For those who are young in spirit, Ammann is a master of putting real everyday people with real nowadays problems beneath the Fairyland costumes. King Cole is un-merry because he has three daughters of marriageable age — and no prospective sons-in-law to take them off his hands. And the King has the problem of all political leaders: "To never be able to admit you are wrong . . . it is a curse." Then there's an old witch who has to fight inflation — the price of bats and lizards has gone out of sight.

Ammann's usual subtle satire is also here. The professional dragon hunter decides to reform; he will never kill an animal again. "From now on," he proclaims, "I shall let the butchers do all the dirty work, like killing. I shall enjoy eating meat and never give another thought how it came about." There is the near-sighted president of the Birdwatchers Club and . . . but part of the fun in reading a playscript is discovering these delights for yourself.

"The Magic Well" can be played by adult actors or by pre-adults of virtually any age. The set may be a simple outdoor scene with cut-out trees and a cardboard well. (See the *'Stage Magic'* Production Script for full details and drawings of set, costumes, props, etc.) Costumes can be of any period, or — like the original production — a kaleidoscope of all periods. After all, the play is as modern as ecology and as old as Fairyland.

"The Magic Well" is the kind of play that *'Stage Magic'* likes to offer — it will help you do enchanting things on your stage.

THE MAGIC WELL

By Herman O. Ammann

moon

[As curtain rises the stage is empty except for the stone well about four feet high at Stage Center. It has four posts and a thatched roof. There are three large rocks to the right and three to the left of the well. These rocks are large enough to sit or stand on. At Down Right is a bench; another just like it is at Down Left. Several trees form a background for the set. Lights are low, for the time is midnight.

The PROLOGUE enters and delivers the following speech, beginning with the tone of a mother telling a fairy tale to a little child.]

PROLOGUE. Once upon a time about a thousand years ago, there was a little village somewhere in Central Europe. I would tell you the name of the village, but it isn't important, and anyway, you never heard of it. In the very center of the village was an old well from which all the villagers got their water. Now that wasn't very unusual except for one thing — *[in a mysterious voice, pointing at the well]* the well, the one you are looking at, was a magic well . . . *[whispering]* and no one in the village knew it! This was a very peaceful and serene community and nothing ever happened. Nothing unusual or exciting had happened for hundreds of years. Really there was no need for a magic well — *[very mysterious]* until one night . . .

[A DRAGON enters Left. He has a horrible head and tail with bumps on the top side. The tail drags behind as he crosses below the well.]

DRAGON. Gronk, gronk, gronk, gronk-gronk-gronk-gronk. *[He moves slowly across the stage saying "gronk" at measured intervals; then interspersing with four or five rapid gronks in a row, as though he was enjoying his midnight stroll. He leaves the stage at Right.]*

2

PROLOGUE. With the arrival of the dragon, the well knew that things in the village would never again be the same. And then came the dawn . . . [PROLOGUE again points toward the stage and — as the lights get brighter and the audience's attention is directed toward the action — backs off and disappears.]

[A man dressed as a KING enters. He sits down on a bench, unrolls a scroll and starts studying it. He takes out a quill, scratches on the paper, writes on it, and in general seems to be engrossed in his composition. Three men — the OLD MAN, the TOWN POET, and the TOWN FOOL — and the OLD WOMAN enter. They are talking excitedly and do not notice the king.]

OLD WOMAN. Mrs. Blinky said she saw one with her own two eyes.

OLD MAN. [Beside the Old Woman, leaning on a gnarled walking stick] Mrs. Blinky can't see the end of her nose.

TOWN FOOL. [Speaking like a dunce] If Mrs. Blinky said she saw a dragon in the big forest, I believe her.

TOWN POET. That's why they call you "Town Fool" and "Bumpkin."

You, Town Fool, have a head like a pumpkin.

[He sits and writes down his immortal words.]

OLD MAN. The Town Poet is right. It is your kind who believes every bit of gossip.

OLD WOMAN. When people hear others' news, they always say it's gossip. If you had heard it first, Old Man, you'd be bragging and believing it a fact for sure.

OLD MAN. Even if it was true, I wouldn't care. They don't make dragons like they used to. The knights killed all the bad ones. Those that are left are shy. Why, Old Woman, they'd never come into the village. They'd be afraid of you!

[OLD WOMAN takes his cane and hits OLD MAN on top of head. He covers up and falls on the ground. TOWN FOOL watches with glee.]

OLD MAN. Stop it, woman, stop it!

THE KING. [Rising] Cease this violence in the street. Stop this caterwauling and flogging in public.

[At the sound of the King's voice, all turn and kneel.]

TOWN POET.   Well, bless my soul;
                It's Old King Cole.
[He writes it down.]
KING COLE. *[Sits]* You'd better believe it, sonny.
OLD WOMAN. Oh, your Majesty, I didn't see you. I would never have beaten my Old Man in public.
OLD MAN. *[Speaks in an aged, whiny voice.]* She always beats me at home. *[Rubs head]* Ow-oo-o-o-oo!
KING COLE. Is this true? Do you beat this old man at home? Where there is no one to see, no one to bear witness?
OLD WOMAN. *[Hangs head until it nearly touches the ground]* I'm afraid I do, your Majesty.
KING COLE. Well then, take him home and beat him. I can't stand his caterwauling. And give him a couple of extra licks for me!

[OLD WOMAN rises, takes OLD MAN by the ear and leads him to Left exit.]

TOWN FOOL. *[Bouncing jubilantly to exit]* I seen the King; I seen the King!
TOWN POET. *[Follows Fool; stops at exit and addresses audience]*   What a democratic feat,
                To meet and greet
                The King on the street.
                But, Dragons, alas!
                What's coming to pass?
[He takes out his pad and jots these immortal lines down as he exits.]

[The KING looks after them, then resumes studying the paper. He makes more corrections. An OLD HAG enters carrying an old black pot in one hand and an old broom in the other. Not recognizing the King, she sits on the bench beside him and drops the pot and broom noisily on the ground. The KING jumps and gives her a dirty look.]

OLD HAG. Am I ever beat. Business is terrible; no one wants me to cast a spell, my feet hurt, and the price of lizards,

4

bats, and snakes has gone out of sight. *[She notices the King for the first time and jabs him in the ribs with her elbow.]* Say, aren't you . . . why I bet you really are that fellow that does all the laughing. What is that name again? I always forget.

KING COLE. *[Looking at her disdainfully]* Old King Cole.

OLD HAG. That's right. Old King Cole. But they call you something else. You've a nickname. Some crazy thing that rhymes.

KING COLE. *[Anything but merry]* The Merry Old Soul.

OLD HAG. That's it. That's the name I was trying to think of. Whoever hung that one on you should be fed to the dragon.

KING COLE. Who else would bestow it except the town poet?

OLD HAG. What are you doing with that paper? You are not acting very merry today. Do you have a king-size hang-up?

KING COLE. I am working on a proclamation which I am going to make from the center balcony tomorrow. *[Rise, importantly]* It is going to be an official edict.

OLD HAG. An edict, eh? Say that is going to be important . . . I will have to be there.

KING COLE. It will be the most important edict I have ever concocted.

OLD HAG. Hey, slow down there a minute, King. I don't even know what an edict is, much less a concocted.

KING COLE. An edict is an official statement which I am making to announce to the public that my three daughters are ready to take husbands.

OLD HAG. You want them out of the house.

KING COLE. Something like that.

OLD HAG. What is the problem . . . each one is prettier than the other?

KING COLE. That's what you think . . . only one of them is pretty. The other two spend all their time and my money in beauty salons.

OLD HAG. This should be a happy time for you. The Queen will take care of the daughters. You have no worries.

KING COLE. You still don't understand. I know they will

all find husbands, but the one that marries first will become the Queen . . . when the wife and I have gone to our rewards. Since we have no son, the dynasty will pass to the first-wed daughter.

OLD HAG. Then the suitor that first takes a wife will be marrying a Queen?

KING COLE. Yes, but he won't know it. It is most important that it be kept a secret.

OLD HAG. A secret that everyone knows is the biggest secret of all.

KING COLE. What does that mean?

OLD HAG. O, King, get smart. Every man thinks he's marrying a queen. *[KING exits. HAG, following, stops, gets idea, comes back onstage.]* What is the matter with me? This is a magic well. Why don't I take advantage of it! I know what I'll do . . . I'll make a magic potion, and between us we'll solve the village problems . . . and a few of my own problems, too! *[Exit excitedly]*

[The OLD MAN, OLD WOMAN, MRS. BLINKY, TOWN POET, and TOWN FOOL enter.]

OLD MAN. Mrs. Blinky, tell us again how you thought you saw a dragon while you were out birdwatching.

MRS. BLINKY. *[She wears very large glasses.]* I didn't think I saw a dragon . . . I did see one . . . big as life! I had just taken note of a Speckled Belly Woodpecker when this enormous creature appeared. He was looking down at me through the boughs. He was bigger than a pachyderm.

TOWN FOOL. What's a pach-y-derm?

OLD MAN. It's an elephant. An animal smaller than a dragon. He has a tail on both ends, and the one in front is bigger!

TOWN FOOL. A tail on both ends, eh? Then how does he know which way he's going?

OLD MAN. It doesn't matter. When you are that big, everything gets out of your way.

[TOWN FOOL retreats to a rock and sits to ponder this statement.]

OLD WOMAN. I heard the King has brought in a professional hunter.

MRS. BLINKY. I think that is terrible. Our Birdwatchers Society is joining with the Society for the Preservation of Dragons in petitioning the king to call off the hunt. Our dragons are an essential part of our heritage.

OLD MAN. I don't think you have anything to worry about. I don't believe you saw a dragon in the first place.

TOWN POET. Well, we won't be long in doubt.
 Here comes the man we've been talking about!

[A handsome young man — PRINCE ARLO MARLOWE — backs in; he appears to be looking at something way off in the forest.]

PRINCE ARLO. I never heard such bellowing in my life. It's not much fun when they act like that.

OLD MAN. What are you talking about? Who are you?

PRINCE ARLO. *[Turns, sees them, switches on the charm]* Oh, excuse me. Permit me to introduce myself. I am Prince Arlo Marlowe. I'm a professional dragon hunter . . . among other things.

OLD MAN. Glad to meet you, sir. I am known as the Old Man in this village, and this is my wife, the Old Woman. *[He indicates each as he introduces them.]* This fellow here is the Town Poet. *[POET bows sumptuously and gracefully. FOOL tries to imitate his bow and nearly falls.]* And that other one, obviously, is the Town Fool. The lady with the large glasses is Mrs. Blinky. She's a bit nearsighted, the head of the local Birdwatching Society and an ardent conservationist.

MRS. BLINKY. What were you talking to yourself about? You mentioned something about some animal crying for help.

PRINCE ARLO. The dragon. *[He looks into the distance offstage; MRS. BLINKY looks with him, peering and blinking through her big glasses.]* I just caught a glimpse of him and hurled my spear. I don't know if I struck a vital spot or not, but he disappeared into the brush bellowing in a rather pitiful manner. I will have to get some dogs and go after him. It was my best spear!

MRS. BLINKY. I am going to get Old King Cole to issue

an edict against dragon hunting.

TOWN FOOL. Speaking of the King, he gave me some sort of paper this morning. *[Holds up a piece of parchment.]* I was supposed to post it on the well. *[He goes over and sticks paper on a nail on the well.]*

MRS. BLINKY. *[Goes to well and begins to read, her nose about three inches from the paper]* "The King's Edict: Be it known throughout this land, my three daughters are ready to be courted and wed. Signed, Old King Cole. P.S. The Merry Old Soul."

PRINCE ARLO. When he hired me, the King didn't mention he had three daughters. I should like to look into this. It sounds interesting.

OLD WOMAN. They are very pretty! But one is prettier than the others.

OLD MAN. All young girls are pretty!

OLD WOMAN. Oh, shut up, you silly Old Man. *[To Arlo]* You can judge for yourself, Prince Arlo . . . here they come now.

[KING and his three DAUGHTERS enter.]

KING COLE. Oh, there you are, Prince Arlo Marlowe. I want you to meet my three daughters: Tissy, Prissy, and Lissy.

TISSY. *[Curtsies prettily]* I'm Tissy; I'm the pretty one.

PRISSY. *[Curtsies cleverly]* I'm Prissy; I'm the clever one.

LISSY. *[Curtsies smartly]* I'm Lissy; I'm the smart one.

PRINCE ARLO. *[Bows gallantly]* Pretty, clever, and smart! I'm glad those traits are split up. I'd hate to find them all in one woman.

KING. You haven't met their mother. She's ugly, sneaky, and dumb.

DAUGHTERS. Father!

PRINCE ARLO. I understand these girls are making their debut.

TOWN POET. 'Tis true, 'tis true,
And watch your step
Or one of them
Will marry you!

[He jerks out his pad and writes it down.]

PRINCE ARLO. I, Sir, came to slay the dragon, but I am not averse to a bit of courtship. It might be more sporting than pursuing a cowardly dragon!

MRS. BLINKY. We were hoping that, as a sportsman, you would be more interested in the preservation of a species than in extermination.

[The OLD HAG enters, sets her pot down, sits on a rock, and begins to stir the pot with the handle of her broom.]

OLD HAG. This village is in a terrible state. The King wants to get his daughters out of the house; the Conservation and Birdwatching Societies want to stop the killing; and the hunter, Prince Arlo Marlowe, has decided to chase girls!

OLD MAN. *[To Old Hag]* I suppose you have an answer to these problems which plague us?

TOWN POET. It's always true
When witches brew
Trouble, trouble,
They stir up double.

[Writes it down]

OLD HAG. I, Sir, am making a magic potion which I shall pour into the well. The well will then solve all problems . . . even romantic ones.

TOWN FOOL. Will it make me smart?

OLD HAG. It certainly can't make you any dumber! I will pour in a little of my brew. *[Pours some in]*

TOWN FOOL. *[Looks in well]* I don't see nothing. *[Listens to well]* I don't hear nothing.

OLD HAG. Perhaps if you would place a coin in my pot . . .

TOWN FOOL. *[He drops a coin in her pot. OLD HAG quickly takes it out, bites it, and places it in her pocket. TOWN FOOL leans over and looks into well; puts hands to ears and listens.]* I still don't see nothing. And I don't hear nothing. *[To her]* I lost my coin!

OLD HAG. You see, it does have magic qualities. You are getting smarter already.

KING COLE. If you are going to charge for the use of the well, I shall have to collect a sales tax.

OLD HAG. Let's not start that. I am just running a small business. I don't want to get involved in a lot of bookkeeping. The well will be free.

KING COLE. *[To Prince Arlo]* Before all this nonsense started, you said something about courting my daughters. How will you know which one to woo?

PRINCE ARLO. It will be a hard decision to make. They are all quite talented. Pretty, clever, and smart. Perhaps the old hag has the answer.

OLD HAG. The Magic Well will answer all questions. But it must have time.

TISSY. *[Daintily]* How long will that be? I am in a hurry. I won't be pretty forever.

PRISSY. *[Imperiously]* It isn't much fun being clever if you don't have a man to fool.

LISSY. *[Casually]* I don't care. If I can't get a man, I can always organize a Women's Liberation Group!

MRS. BLINKY. There are too many organizations in this village now. You should join one of the established ones like the Birdwatchers.

LISSY. A nearsighted birdwatcher that can't see anything smaller than a dragon!

MRS. BLINKY. You could do worse. You're always acting so smart. A person can be too smart . . . especially a woman. *[The PRINCESSES exit. MRS. BLINKY follows them off.]*

OLD MAN. Let's stop arguing among ourselves. I don't believe this old well has any magic powers, but in the face of such indecision maybe we should give it a try.

KING COLE. I will issue an edict. The well has until sunrise tomorrow to solve all our problems; otherwise I shall order it filled with sticks and stones.

OLD HAG. Ah, it is getting late and the sun sets in the west. I shall sit here all night stirring my pot.

OLD MAN. Come on, old woman. Let's be getting back to the house.

OLD WOMAN. That's the first thing you said today that makes sense. All this talk about magic and dragons — it gives me the creeps. *[They exit.]*

TOWN FOOL. Witches and goblins and dragons! I'm scared that if I stay here I will get scared! *[Exit]*

PRINCE ARLO. It's easy to see why they call him the Town Fool. Still . . . there is something amiss. I think I'll just hide in the shadows and see what happens this night. *[Hides behind a tree]*

    TOWN POET. *[Stands on a rock, orates]*
        The sun now sinks into the West,
        And I must leave with all the rest.
        But ere I go, I want to say:
        [to well] Please don't let me down today.
        Please, oh, please don't let us down.
        Why . . . you're the only well in town! *[He takes out his pad and writes these words down as he exits.]*

    [Lights go down low except for a spot on well.]

    OLD HAG. The moon is full. That will be a lot of help.

    PRINCE ARLO. *[Coming out from behind the tree]* Most romantic problems are solved at night. That is . . . when the moon is bright!

    OLD HAG. Now, you are going to have to remain quiet or the well can't work its magic. *[Noise offstage left]* Hark . . . someone is coming! Be still.

    DRAGON. *[Off left]* Gronk! Grrr . . . ONK! Grr. . . onk! *[DRAGON enters. There is a spear sticking in his tail. He staggers to Stage Center, his cries becoming weaker.]* Grrr . . . onk! Grrr . . . onk. Ohhh, Gronk! *[He collapses on the ground.]*

    PRINCE ARLO. Why, it's the dragon. He still has my spear in his tail. What a terrible way to die. What a horrible thing I have done, to cause a creature to go off and die in the middle of the night.

    OLD HAG. There isn't any doubt about it. His life is ebbing away.

    PRINCE ARLO. We must do something. We must help him. *[But he stands there helpless, not knowing what to do.]*

    OLD HAG. That is the way with you hunters. You want to slay things, but you don't like to see the blood.

    PRINCE ARLO. You don't understand. I never meant it to be like this. I wanted to make a clean kill. This is no good. The meat will be spoiled. If there were just something that could be done . . .

    OLD HAG. Perhaps the Magic Well . . .

PRINCE ARLO. Stop your nonsense, Old Hag, we aren't playing games here. This calls for action. But what to do? The poor fellow is going fast. He hardly breathes, much less gronks.

MRS. BLINKY. *[Off left]* Wait a minute! Wait a minute! *[She runs on carrying a large white bandage and a bit of small rope.]* Hold tight. Don't give up. Hang in there, baby. Mrs. Blinky will help you. *[She pulls at spear.]* If I could just extract this weapon. *[Sees Prince Arlo]* Oh, it's you, you terrible man. Help me with this instrument of torture. *[They pull on the spear and finally get it out. They throw it on the ground near the well.]*

PRINCE ARLO. I am very sorry. I had no idea. Do you think he is . . . I mean . . . has he . . . passed away?

MRS. BLINKY. *[Bends over to listen for heartbeat]* I don't think so. I can detect a faint heartbeat. Perhaps a bit of water from the well to cleanse the wound. Get the dipper there.

PRINCE ARLO. *[He goes to well, takes dipper from one of the posts and fills it. He brings it to MRS. BLINKY, who pours it over the wound. The DRAGON stirs, pushes tail back and forth a bit.]* He's stirring. He's moving his tail. I do believe he is recovering.

DRAGON. Oh! Oh! Oh! Oh, GRONK!

MRS. BLINKY. Here, help me bandage the wound. The water from the well seems to have some magical powers. *[PRINCE ARLO helps her.]*

PRINCE ARLO. I didn't know these lowly creatures could suffer.

MRS. BLINKY. And why not? Don't you think dragons have feelings, the same as people? If you stick things into them, they too will cry out in their agony.

PRINCE ARLO. It's just that I never gave it much thought.

MRS. BLINKY. You hunters never think.

PRINCE ARLO. You are right, Mrs. Blinky. From now on I shall let the butchers do all the dirty work, like killing. I shall enjoy eating meat and never give another thought how it came about.

DRAGON. *[Sitting up, quite recovered]* I want to thank you good people for helping me in my distress.

PRINCE ARLO. Well, I'll be. A talking dragon!

DRAGON. I don't usually talk, but I am so thankful. I was beginning to think there were only kooks in this village. I am glad to learn you can be kind and gentle. *[Starts off.]*

MRS. BLINKY. Where are you going? What will you do?

DRAGON. I am going to another part of the forest. Far away from here. Half the people here want to kill me and the other half want to put me on the birthday calendar. From now on I shall eat only herbs. *[He exits. After a moment we hear a GRONK of freedom disappearing into the forest.]*

MRS. BLINKY. See what a wonderful fellow he turned out to be. Imagine that: an herbivorous dragon! *[She leaves.]*

OLD HAG. Get back in the shadows, Prince Arlo. The night is young. *[PRINCE ARLO returns to his tree.]*

TISSY. *[Enters]* Oh, hello there, Old Hag. Why are you up so late?

OLD HAG. I am going to spend the night stirring my pot and pouring magic potions into the well. Aren't you one of the King's daughters?

TISSY. *[Sweetly, sincerely — completely without affectation or pride]* Yes, I am Tissy; I'm the pretty one. I am so pretty I am afraid to look into a mirror. I get goose bumps.

OLD HAG. You certainly are pretty, all right. Tell me, dear, do you have any brains?

TISSY. Brains? Who needs them?

OLD HAG. I thought you wanted to get married! It would help if you had a brain.

TISSY. You know, no one ever asks me out. They all admire me, but they are afraid of me because of my beauty. Really, sometimes it is like a curse.

OLD HAG. I wouldn't know about that. I've never had that problem.

TISSY. *[Almost in tears]* What does a person do? I mean besides sit around and look pretty?

OLD HAG. I don't know, but I am getting a little tired of listening to your drivel. You sure your name's Tissy and not Narcissy?

TISSY. No, I'm just pretty little old me — Tissy!

OLD HAG. Oh, button your lip.

TISSY. Oh, me, oh, me. I do wish I could get married. But,

of course, he would have to be a Prince. *[Notices spear on ground]* What is this? Why it's an old spear. People shouldn't leave dangerous weapons around like this. It's probably not even registered. I will throw it into the well. *[She throws spear into well. There is a "Grrr . . . ump, grrr . . . UMP!" TISSY runs to Old Hag and holds on to her for protection.]*

OLD HAG. My goodness! Don't tell me there is another dragon in the well!

TISSY. Another what?

OLD HAG. Never mind. Didn't you hear something?

TISSY. I most certainly did. I — *[From the well: "GRRR . . . UMP"]* There, I heard it again. *[A large FROG's head emerges from the top of the well.]* Why, it's a frog!

OLD HAG. It sure isn't a dog, or a hog, or a log!

FROG. Grrr . . . ump. Grrr . . . ump. Grrr . . . ump. Kiss me! Kiss me! Kiss me!

TISSY. What an ugly thing to say: to ask someone as pretty as me . . . to kiss thee. *[FROG sinks back into well.]*

OLD HAG. Well, you said yourself, no one ever asked you out. You should be more friendly. After all, everyone can't be pretty.

TISSY. A frog? Are you suggesting that I kiss a frog? A slippery, slimy, slithering saurian?

FROG. *[Reappearing]* A slithering saurian? Baby, I am no saurian, and I don't slither. If you want to get technical, you might refer to me as a tailess, leaping, hopping amphibian.

OLD HAG. He means he is a FROG . . . and ALL FROG!

TISSY. I can see what he is. *[Backing away, toward R]* He is disgusting.

FROG. Grrr . . . ump. Grrr . . . ump. Kiss me! Kiss me! You won't be sorry.

TISSY. Well! I am not going to stay around another minute and listen to a fresh fellow like you. *[She leaves.]*

OLD HAG. I didn't know you were in the well. I am amazed.

PRINCE ARLO. *[Emerges from shadows]* What is going on, Old Hag? Who are you talking to? *[FROG sinks into well.]*

14

OLD HAG. Just an old friend. You wouldn't believe it if I told you.

PRINCE ARLO. Try me.

OLD HAG. You will find out soon enough. It is quite possible our problems will be solved before the rising of the sun.

PRINCE ARLO. Some mighty queer things are happening this night. Here comes another of those daughters; I believe it is Prissy, the clever one. [PRINCE ARLO returns to shadows. PRISSY appears.]

OLD HAG. Hello, Miss Prissy.

PRISSY. Hello yourself, Old Hag. Has the Magic Well worked any wonders yet?

OLD HAG. You could say that, yes. A dragon came by. He was in distress from a wound. He had a spear sticking in his tail, but Prince Arlo Marlowe and Mrs. Blinky extracted the weapon. They cleansed the wound with water from the well and the dragon recovered immediately.

PRISSY. Are you insinuating that the well really does have some magic quality?

OLD HAG. I am not insinuating any such thing. I am merely stating facts. Then there is another thing that even I did not know.

PRISSY. And what is that?

OLD HAG. There is something living in the well.

PRISSY. A snake, a turtle, a very large spider?

OLD HAG. No, it's a frog. An extremely interesting and unusual frog.

PRISSY. A frog's a frog; a dog's a dog; and a log's a log.

OLD HAG. Don't you start that. You had better take this particular frog seriously for he is likely to be the most important frog you will ever meet.

PRISSY. I am more interested in the magic qualities of the water in the well.

FROG. [In the well] Grrr... ump. Grrr...ump.Gr...ump.

PRISSY. [Startled] What is that? It sounds like a frog!

OLD HAG. It should, dearie.

PRISSY. Then there really is a frog in there. I shall have to get him out. He will contaminate the well! [Peers into the

well] Hello, down there. Come up here. You must get out of the well. *[FROG appears; PRISSY backs away a few steps.]*

FROG. Grrr . . . ump. Grrr. . . ump.Grrr. . . ump. Kiss me! Kiss me!

PRISSY. He talks! He talks! You are right. He is a very unusual frog. But what an odd thing for him to say.

OLD HAG. He asks everyone that. He asked your sister Tissy a while ago.

PRISSY. Did she kiss him? I mean she's very dumb; it's quite possible she did. You know she never has any dates.

OLD HAG. You shouldn't be putting your sister down like that.

PRISSY. What I mean is, she isn't clever like me. She is very anxious. She'd probably go out with anyone if they'd just ask. Not many people are clever like me.

OLD HAG. I've heard that. You are always trying to figure out a different way to do something. You want to outfigure everyone else.

PRISSY. If you were clever, you would have figured this out: here we have a well with magic water; and as if that weren't enough, we also have a talking frog.

OLD HAG. I am getting a premonition that your cleverness will not be used for the public's advantage. You are contemplating commercialization of two natural wonders! Shame on you!

PRISSY. Shame on yourself. You and your lizards, bats, and snakes. Who are you to be so high and mighty?

OLD HAG. Hold on there, little girl. I didn't tell you everything. You have a lot to learn.

PRISSY. Oh, forget it. I'm going to get my sister Lissy. She is the smart one. Together we will find a way to make a lot of money with the frog and the well. *[She leaves.]*

PRINCE ARLO. *[Emerging from the shadows]* She certainly does like money, doesn't she!

OLD HAG. Yes, her father has plenty, but she isn't satisfied. People who are not needy shouldn't be greedy.

PRINCE ARLO. You phrased it very well. Why, a person like that could upset the whole economy of this village.

OLD HAG. Tourists, sightseers, people by the hundreds

would come to see the frog and the well.

PRINCE ARLO. People by the thousands!

OLD HAG. They would spend a lot of money.

PRINCE ARLO. The village would become the richest in the district!

OLD HAG. Gold pieces would litter the streets!

PRINCE ARLO. We could sell souvenirs, postcards, bottle the water!

OLD HAG. A fortune could be made!

PRINCE ARLO. Let's get our share! Let's try to get it all!!

OLD HAG. *[Turning her back on him; sadly]* How quickly money corrupts.

PRINCE ARLO. *[Turns his back on her]* You are right. I just happened to have that little thought for a brief moment.

OLD HAG. To not want to get rich is a constant battle.

PRINCE ARLO. Yes . . . but most people seem to win it.

OLD HAG. It is one of life's easier battles.

FROG. I still wish someone would kiss me.

PRINCE ARLO. Oh, shut up and go back down in your well.

FROG. Well, all right, but I too have my little thoughts . . . my dreams.

PRINCE ARLO. And what gem of wisdom would you be capable of?

FROG. That to want to be loved is more important than to want riches.

OLD HAG. Ah, yes. We live in a complicated world. But then, I am afraid it is the people themselves who complicate it! *[She sits and stirs her brew; FROG descends into well.]*

PRINCE ARLO. I have just noticed that it's almost time for sunrise. The King will be here soon.

OLD HAG. Yes, time is running out.

PRINCE ARLO. Do you really think the King will fill the well with sticks and stones?

OLD HAG. The King is a very proud man. In order to maintain his pride, he will have to keep his vow.

PRINCE ARLO. His vow?

OLD HAG. Yes, when the King makes an edict, it is the same as a Royal Vow. Nothing can change his mind.

PRINCE ARLO. But the well. It was expecting too much of an inanimate object. No one is perfect.

OLD HAG. Look, Arlo, I have been stirring this pot all night. I have done all I can. What have you done, besides eavesdropping on other people?

PRINCE ARLO. I have learned a lot. I am a changed man since the Dragon thing. And you know something else? I have a most peculiar feeling about the old well.

OLD HAG. You have learned to love it.

PRINCE ARLO. Yes, it has become very dear to me. And even the frog. You know, for a frog, he isn't a bad fellow at all. You can't blame him for wanting to be loved.

OLD HAG. That is true, and I rather imagine to another frog he would be quite beautiful; but really, from you I am a bit surprised!

PRINCE ARLO. Oh, you know what I mean. Every creature should be respected for what it is. Now you take a frog and a dog and a . . .

OLD HAG. Oh, cut that out. You, too?

PRINCE ARLO. It's about over. It is very sad. Here comes the King and just about everyone else.

[All the rest of the cast except the Dragon, Prissy, and Lissy enter. Each one has a bundle of sticks and a large rock, which he deposits near the well.]

KING COLE. All right, you people, put your sticks and stones over by the well. *[Notices Arlo]* Oh, hello, Prince Arlo, and you, Old Hag. The well didn't do a thing, did it! It let us down. Well, I figured as much. Still, I issued the edict, the proclamation. I must keep the Royal Vow. The old saying is true: Heavy hangs the head that wears the crown. *[Shakes head]* The sun is almost risen. When it does — goodbye, well.

PRINCE ARLO. You know, I think the King is quite sad. He seems shaken. I bet he wishes something would happen; but, of course, nothing will.

OLD HAG. I say there, Mr. King Cole, the well did show magic powers during the night. It cured the dragon, and he has left the district promising never to return.

KING COLE. But there were other things: the state of the economy, and those three daughters — they are still around my house.

PRINCE ARLO. Perhaps if you would admit you acted hastily . . . we all love the well. I feel even you harbor a certain affinity.

KING COLE. To never be able to admit you are wrong . . . it is a curse!

TISSY. To be pretty . . . it, too, is a curse.

PRINCE ARLO. I guess everyone has ended up cursed. After all, I turned chicken in the middle of the hunt.

TOWN POET. *[Standing on a rock]*
>To live in this world
>Is a wonder unfurled
>When things are going good.
>But when things go bad
>It is very sad.
>The Well did all it could! *[He continues to stand on the rock, like a Greek god, writing his words on his tablet.]*

KING COLE. I could settle the state of the economy. The fact is, it wasn't very good in the first place; but my daughters' hands unsolicited . . . it is a blow to the Royal Pride!

OLD MAN. You mean it is time to fill the well?

KING COLE. I am afraid so. *[He snaps his fingers; they all begin picking up their bundles of sticks and stones.]*

LISSY. *[Off]* Wait a minute, Father. I am coming. *[Enters rapidly]* I hope that I am not too late. *[Turns to PRISSY, who accompanies her]* And I hope you have been telling me the truth.

PRISSY. I swear it is true. I have a witness. The Old Hag saw it too!

MRS. BLINKY. What did you see? I didn't see anything. *[She peers anxiously around the stage, very near-sighted.]*

OLD MAN. You never see anything . . . except dragons!

TOWN FOOL. She seen the dragon all right. You made fun of her and she seen it. You ought to be ashamed.

KING COLE. *[To Prissy]* What are you talking about?

PRISSY. There is a frog in the well.

KING COLE. So, my dear, there is a frog in the well. Do

you know something? I never did like frogs very well anyway.

LISSY. Father, you don't understand. The frog is the answer to all our problems.

KING COLE. I am running out of patience. First I put my faith in an Old Hag that claims to be a witch. Now you want me to believe a frog? No wonder you can't find a husband! Who would want a nut like you?

LISSY. You all have a lot to learn. The reason I am known as the smart one is because I read a lot. Don't you know there are stories, dozens of stories, about frogs? A lot of them live in rivers, lakes, and a few, like this fellow here, live in wells. They have curses on them.

OLD HAG. I didn't think anyone else knew. Not very many people do.

MRS. BLINKY. A magic frog?

TOWN FOOL. I bought a magic goose one time.

OLD MAN. I don't remember anything about that.

TOWN FOOL. Yep, I sure did. I bought him from a fellow named Jack. He was a fellow that grew beanstalks. He had this here beanstalk that climbed way up into the sky. One day he climbed it and there was a castle and a giant and Jack, he . . .

OLD MAN. Yes, yes, we know all about that. What about the magic goose?

TOWN FOOL. He told me it laid golden eggs.

OLD MAN. And did it?

TOWN FOOL. Nope, he lied to me. I never got nothing but goose eggs. Hee, hee, hee, haw, haw, haw.

OLD WOMAN. We have given him the wrong name. Instead of calling him the Town Fool, we should have been calling him the Village Idiot!

LISSY. *[Into the well]* Say, Mr. Frog. Come up here.

FROG. *[In well]* Grrr . . . ump. Grrr . . . ump.

LISSY. Don't be bashful. The time has come. *[FROG appears.]* Stop your grrr. . . umping and pop the question!

FROG. I was getting discouraged. Do you really want me to?

LISSY. You'd better believe your green britches. You see, I know your secret.

FROG. I have waited so long! Kiss me, kiss me, kiss me!

[LISSY leans forward to kiss him, but the KING stops her with the following speech.]
KING COLE. Just a minute here. I have something to say about this. Are you actually intending to kiss that frog?
LISSY. Father, I might as well tell you now. This really isn't a frog.
KING COLE. It'll do until a real one comes along. Stop your nonsense. I'll not have a frog around the house for a son-in-law!
LISSY. It isn't really a frog. An old legend I was reading tells all about it. Many years ago a handsome prince was bewitched and turned into a frog. He has had to live in this old well for a hundred years. When I kiss him, he will be released from the curse and turn back into a handsome young prince!
KING COLE. *[To audience]* She wants to kiss a frog! Where have I failed?
TOWN POET. *[Still standing on rock like a Greek god]*
There's one thing to bear in mind:
He may be rich, and not unkind.
So he doesn't have a hank of hair . . .
In the eyes of frogs, he's debonair!
Oh, what a perfectly beautiful sign:
Lovers of frogs . . . need to be blind!
[Writes it down]
LISSY. *[Leans over to frog]* Come, dear. Pucker up. Kiss me, sweetie! *[They kiss.]*
FROG. *[Hopping out of well]* Oh, thank you for breaking the evil spell and getting me out of that dark dank well.
LISSY. It's all right now, darling, it's all over.
FROG. *[Starts leap-frogging toward exit]* Yes, it is all over, and I want you to know I appreciate your kindness.
LISSY. Just a minute. Where are you going? And when are you going to turn into a handsome prince?
FROG. Are you joking? You have been reading too many fairy stories. This isn't make-believe. It's reality. A frog's a frog, a dog's a dog, and a log's a log.
OLD HAG. Not you, too. Why — you really are a frog!
FROG. Of course I'm a frog. And I intend to spend the

rest of my life with other frogs. People disgust me. Besides
. . . *[wipes mouth]* they are lousy lovers. *[Hops offstage.]*

[LISSY faints and the KING catches her. OLD MAN gets dipper of water, pours it on LISSY, who promptly revives.]

KING COLE. What an evil well. Fill it up! It has insulted the Royal Family!

PRINCE ARLO. Hold it. Just a minute, King Cole. It is time I made my move and saved the well.

OLD MAN. What do you intend to do?

PRINCE ARLO. I am going to marry one of the King's daughters.

KING COLE. You are? *[Shakes his hand]* Why, my son, that is wonderful. It will solve all our problems. Even save the well.

[The PRINCESSES line up, each confident that she will be chosen.]

OLD MAN AND THE REST. Hurrah for Prince Arlo Marlowe!

KING COLE. Just a moment. Which one did you pick? *[Pointing to Lissy and Prissy]* The smart one or the clever one?

PRINCE ARLO. *[Steps to the girls, looks them over]* Neither. I have decided to marry Tissy. *[Gallantly kneels before her and takes her hand]*

KING COLE. My son, you have picked the dumb one!

PRINCE ARLO. Dumb to you, perhaps, but not to me. *[Rise, releasing her hand and facing the king]* You see, I am not too smart myself. Every time I look at Tissy, I will feel superior.

TISSY. *[Takes his arm and gazes at him admiringly]* Oh, Prince Arlo. You are so handsome and smart. I think you are just wonderful!

PRINCE ARLO. *[To audience]* See what I mean!

KING COLE. *[Striding around the stage happily, addressing the crowd]* That does it. Throw away your sticks and stones. You may keep your Magic Well. I am sure the tourist trade will bolster the economy. And, as for my other daughters, if

Prissy is so clever, and Lissy is so smart, they can find their own husbands. And that is the end of it!

OLD HAG. Not quite. You have forgotten something, Old King Cole.

KING COLE. *[Merrily]* Ho, ho, ho. You are quite right, my dear. *[Sits on bench, king-like]* Fetch me my pipe, and fetch me my bowl, and . . . oh yes, get hold of those three fellows around town who are always . . . fiddling around!

CURTAIN

The Bridge

A Fable in One Act by FORD AINSWORTH

Based on "Three Billy Goats Gruff," this play by the author of *Persephone* depicts three trolls who stand guard at a bridge.

On one side of the bridge is a lush green pasture. On the other side is a herd of starving goats. The trolls will not let the goats cross the bridge . . . and the stream beneath is said to have evil consequences for anyone who dares touch its waters.

Three goats come to the bridge to plead with the trolls to let the starving herd cross over to the green pastures. The trolls, who say they are hungry for goat flesh, agree to let the herd cross the bridge on one condition—that a goat be sacrificed to the trolls.

Each of the three goats at the bridge is brave and self-less until it is suggested that he be the sacrifice.

The play points an accusing finger at people who are willing to sacrifice for the nation's good as long as it's the other fellow who does the sacrificing.

A timely play for all groups. Excellent for contests.

6 characters, male or female.

Order from

I. E. CLARK, Inc.
Saint John's Road * Suite AS
Schulenburg, TX 78956